NUMEROLOGY

ITS PRACTICAL APPLICATION TO LIFE

By CLIFFORD W. CHEASLEY

Author of "WHATS IN YOUR NAME"

"LIFE AN INDIVIDUAL PROBLEM" etc.

Editor of "NUMEROLOGY MONTHLY";

Teacher of the Scientific and Consistent

PHILOSOPHY OF NUMBERS.

THIRD EDITION 1921
REVISED

PUBLISHED by THE AUTHOR

337 WEST 23rd STREET

CITY OF NEW YORK

CHAPTERS

1—WHAT IS NUMEROLOGY?

2—THE NUMBERS.

3—CONSTRUCTIVE AND DESTRUCTIVE ASPECTS.

4—NEGATIVE ASPECTS.

5—WHAT YOUR NAME MEANS.

6—NAME DIGITS—EACH NUMBER—SURNAME.

7—WHAT THE BIRTH DATE INDICATES.

8—CHANGING NAMES—SIGNATURES—CHOOSING NAMES.

9—HIDDEN DESIRE OF EACH VIBRATION.

10—HARMONIOUS ASSOCIATION.

11—COUNTRIES, CITIES, HOUSES.

12—LIKELY OCCUPATIONS.

13—WHAT TO DO EACH DAY.

14—NUMBERS AND PERSONALITY.

FOREWORD

In presenting this, the third edition of "NUMEROLOGY, ITS PRACTICAL APPLICATION TO LIFE," I take the opportunity of sincerely thanking hundreds of readers in all parts of the world who have voluntarily expressed their appreciation of the first and second editions.

There is "nothing new under the Sun," and one of the oldest things is the Universal language of Numbers of which NUMEROLOGY is simply the more psychological interpretation, just as mathematics, taught and used in the practical world, is the physical development.

It continues to be my ideal to present NUMEROLOGY in its inclusive simplicity of a Science that explains every expression of Life and Character. I use in my personal work and in the preparation of my writings, revelations of which minds beside my own have been the recording instruments, and also knowledge resulting from years of experience as a teacher, lecturer and counsellor.

Consistency of interpretation is the only superior claim I make for my development of this very ancient but always modern Science; to be successful in establishing in the student's mind definite fundamental principles which, when applied, produce an immediate and convincing result, is the aim of my activity. To appear as the author of some new brand of Number Symbolism, of which there are many that are unable to stand the test of usefulness and fail at the demand of human need. means nothing to me.

NUMEROLOGY, to me means, HUMANOLOGY. For this reason I can, after slight revision, again place this book in the hands of the public confident that it will prove an inspiration and a revelation to many.

Yours in Unity and Service

Clifford Cheasley

NUMEROLOGY

CHAPTER I

WHAT IS NUMEROLOGY?

Numerology is simply an extended study of vibration.

Vibration is life and all life is vibrating. Everything is intelligent and intelligence. There is not a single dead or inanimate thing in the Universe, because everything that exists is a manifestation of Energy. Even a chair, which might generally be considered to be without life, is really full of a finer expression of living, vibrating energy, its electrons held together by the laws of attraction which give to it an individuality as distinct upon its own plane as our human personality. Physical science calls this attractive force Cohesion.

Man is the highest point or manifestation of energy in the earth currents and he has included in his journey from the atomic to the human kingdom all the vibratory lessons of the mineral, vegetable, and animal, to which his positive control of all kingdoms of energy bears witness.

In the human vibrations there are many divisions through which man passes and repasses toward that stage where he can be removed from the earth currents and function in a higher consciousness to contact a cycle of new vibratory experiences. The experience which man collects through this passing and repassing builds character and gives individuality to every man and woman at the same time, since it causes the complexities of human nature, which to the average person are contradictory and uncharted.

Little is known of the origin of the Science that claims to interpret man by deciding his place in the human vibratory zones. As far as can be gathered from fragmentary records, little, if any, attention was paid to what we today consider the practical or general interpretation of Number Vibration. Symbology, encouraged by priestcraft, was woven around the subject, and we see this use of the Science made by the Chinese, Persians, Egyptians and Greeks.

It was to Greece, about four centuries B. C. that Pythagoras, a native of Samos, returned from his travels with the foundation of what is known as the Pythagorean Philosophy of Numbers based upon the "Laws of Opposites."

Pythagoras, if we should be consistent and work out his name by our present system of calculation, would be found to be a very practical teacher, and this probably constitutes the reason why, among all the mysticism that surrounded the revelation of Numbers, he was able to find definite principles which could be made into a practical system of philosophy. That he succeeded in building around these few principles a scientific system is evidenced by the fragments of his teachings left to the world.

The world is indebted to him for its present system of music which is based upon the same laws of progression and periodicity that are the foundation of modern NUMEROLOGY in its interpretation of character and circumstance. He left us the evolutionary cycle of 1 to 9 in which he claimed all expressions of human life were revolving.

In common with the early philosophers, Pythagoras never wrote a book, and any fragmentary records of his students were purposely destroyed that they might not fall into the hands of those who would misuse their wisdom. We do know, however, that he was teaching the world a philosophy similar to our "New Thought," having only one substance and that substance God or Good, from which all life and expression emanated, and of which the numbers 1 to 9 were the symbols.

His fundamental of God, the Universal creative force, however, caused him to employ in instructing his pupils in number vibration, the principle that is still maintained of placing the number 1 at the head of all vibration as typifying Creation, God, The One in All and through all, The Supreme Being, The First Cause, etc.; again, in explaining the number 2 as an emanation of the one, or the plane of experience, and 3 as the perfect realization and culmination of the 1 and 2, making in all the perfect trinity of life and creation.

We know that the completed system of number vibration as taught by Pythagoras extended into tens and hundreds, but that it was really founded upon the fundamental vibrations of 1 to 9 already mentioned; so by simply confining ourselves to the cycle of 1 to 9 in our study, we can get results that are absolutely satisfactory for all practical purposes and through which can be carried any interpretation of individual, condition, place or circumstance we wish to make.

"All life is a means to an end, and that end God Consciousness, or consciousness of the

Whole," New Thought tells us; "all life is followed through creation, experience, expression and inclusion."

As the Science of Numerology is studied it will be seen how this is explained even in the simpler expressions of daily life. Every thought we think is a creation, every action along the line of that thought is an experience, every repetition of that act is an expression, and when we seem to surrender that creation for another, it becomes an inclusion—an element of our character for all time.

In our journey from the first stages of human unfoldment we have lived many lives in various colors and conditions, and every condition of every life that we have created for ourselves has followed this process of creation, experience, expression and inclusion before it has been rated as a lesson of the past in our cosmic registration —our baptismal names. It is not hard to believe that we are automatically born and re-born into conditions that will give us our next step on the path to "Consciousness of the Whole." Every family provides a different experience, and the experiences given us by our own family and associates in any life become our expressions and inclusions in succeeding incarnations.

Thus through desire for "consciousness of the whole" we create for ourselves all the associations and opportunities from incarnation to incarnation, experience and express the conditions which they have to offer us, until we find a new creation as the result of the understanding of our own Names and Numbers and recognize our name as a record of our past desires fulfilled and unfulfilled.

It is always interesting to study ourselves and to learn why we do certain things, why we neglect others, why certain expressions appeal to us, and why others do not; our purpose in life, and anything that will increase our happiness and usefulness by revealing our place in the divine plan, and what we really have to do to unfold us the most in our cosmic and human journey, than to study the "inanimate" things around us; although because we confine ourselves more to human expression, it must not be overlooked that this study can and does teach us to understand the expression of *everything* that exists.

Although we are truly in an age when men, as never before, are becoming interested in a study of the self, there are still comparatively few who are able to use this study intelligently in their every-day life. This is not because of unwillingness to take advantage of everything that tends to better their position or increase their understanding, but simply because there has never been a form of study practical enough to be learned and used unless the individual had the time or opportunity to learn first a variety of signs and symbols that—although the foundation of studies which in themselves are truth and which help him materially to know and relate himself—are too unfamiliar to be easily committed to memory or applied when most needed.

It will be readily seen how great is the need that NUMEROLOGY supplies and the reason that it constitutes the most fundamental study of the self that exists today. Its roots are just the numbers 1 to 9, used in conjunction with the letters of the alphabet, which everyone learned in childhood. Once the explanations of the numbers given in the following chapters and elsewhere have been learned, and the simple rules complied with, the study is easily acquired and successfully applied by anyone, although, as in everything else, "practice makes perfect."

The usefulness of NUMEROLOGY, or, as it is generally named in its limited form, "Names and Numbers," is quickly understood.

NUMEROLOGY is also a science that even the younger generation can be brought to use as something to help them recognize their own expressions in the coming contact with others, while adults can use it to great advantage to help understand the expressions they find around them on the path, and as a means of increasing their usefulness and success in every situation of life.

Wherever the numbers are found they carry the same characteristics and will reveal the expression, the inner force and hidden desire of everything to which they are applied.

CHAPTER II

THE NUMBERS

The Numbers, 1, 2, 3, 4, 5, 6, 7, 8, 9, go to make a complete cycle of vibration at any and every point of expression on this earth plane. When these numbers are fully understood they explain to us every possible expression in the material Universe, whether on the mineral, vegetable, animal or human planes.

Each of these numbers existing as a universal cosmic force is neither constructive nor destructive, but shows a neutral force agreeing with the explanations under "General Characteristics" that appear later in this chapter. Therefore it is well to dispel from our minds the belief in "bad" or "unlucky" numbers, for they are all good and lucky in themselves. If we know enough about them we can keep those around our life that harmonize with our own numberscope and thus bring ourselves into relationships where our "luck" or happiness lies.

It will be seen that the 1 to 9 includes odd and even numbers. One of the first fundamentals that we can take into our study is that the odd numbers vibrate harmoniously to the intuitional, feminine or creative side of life expressed through art, literature, science, religion, etc., and that the even numbers vibrate to the intellectual, masculine, receptive side of life expressed through commerce, construction, finance, domesticity, sport, etc.

Beyond the general force of each vibration there *is* constructive and destructive action. These are developed by the life spark in every expression in the material Universe or the "God in all and through all" manifesting in conscious choice and the power of individual creation.

This explains that although in the vibration of dog, there is nothing to show constructive or destructive action, yet in looking at the expression of dog consciousness we find "good" and "bad" dogs just as we find "good" and "bad" men.

The human plane being the highest in the vibratory expressions, man has the power to develop the vibrations of all other earth planes into constructive or destructive action; this is borne out by two humans who will bend to their wills in opposite directions the resources of the same plane of expression.

Constructive action on any plane is just what its name implies, unfolding and evolving into higher vibratory expression; destructive action is the tearing down and destroying of existing expressions and the open doorway that leads to the third aspect of vibration—Negativity.

This last aspect—Negativity—is the point reached in vibratory expression following immediately after the destructive or downward action, and before the new, constructive or upward action is re-commenced.

In the interpretation of human expression it is the position of many individuals whose characters contain high vibrations but are born into environments or forced into circumstances where through bodily or practical limitation their possibilities are kept dormant, awaiting new stimuli to constructive action.

When individuals grow weary of situations that do not really express them, and yet hold day by day before the eyes of their inner consciousness the vision of the situations that do, they are creating a new constructive expression for the future. Creation is made also by condemnation and resistance, but only in the destructive; by acceptance, despondency or pacivity the individual remains in the negative or neutral aspect.

Only a hair's breadth divides the constructive from the destructive aspect. This is often spanned unconsciously by the individual who, not otherwise destructive, finds so many methods that have proven successful for the direction of his own life, and in his desire to benefit his neighbors, forces these methods upon them without due consideration for their individual capacity to receive. From this it is only a short step to constant self-destruction as the result of limiting other's freedom and having his good intentions and advice cast back upon him. Good intentions will not avoid destructive development (the road to hell is paved with them) unless they are directed toward those who by their receptive attitude show that they are ready to be helped.

Thus we have General Aspects, which are always expressed apart from the constructive, destructive and negative aspects; constructive aspects which are the development of the General into its highest possibility; Destructive Aspects which are the development of the General towards destructive action, the misuse of Man's power of creation; and Negative Aspects which result from previous Destructive action. At this point man is again given the opportunity to create higher development.

GENERAL ASPECTS

1. CREATION. All expression originates with the 1, one thought, one word, one cell, etc.; therefore, to put individual expression under this number calls for the necessity of personal creation or the building of individuality. It gives individualization, self-assertiveness, the ability to act as a pioneer and follow individual reasons.

It cannot be expressed through too close attachment to individuals and conditions, but stands for the law of discards that it may make constant unity with new situations and draw material for building.

2. COLLECTION stands for the mixer and is the collector in that it links life with all kinds of individuals and conditions. Reflective, easily moulded into the expressions of individual or condition around it; receptive rather than creative. The peacemaker, the unobstrusive individual, seldom successful upon individual effort. The base upon which many broader public expressions are built, although always in the background, responsible for the finest, smallest details.

3. EXPRESSION. Personal expression, perfection and adornment; artistic, critical, observant. The composite of the 1 and the 2; has added to the individuality of the 1, the experiences of

the 2 and is attempting to realize perfect culmination through ambition for the benefits of this earth plane. Ambition. Entertainment. Society. Style. Inspiration. Individual work.

This vibration is always necessary to the success of the vibrations of 1 and 2, and is in a degree incomplete without either or both of these vibrations on which to rely.

4. MATERIALITY. Uninspirational. Close attention to technicality and physical and mental work. Passing up proofs of ability on the material, mental planes, with very little recognition. Home. Patrotism. Fact. Endurance. Application. The number that makes the conception of spiritual and inspirational expressions difficult. Successful wage earner. Dislike of social obligations. Positive. Physical. Practical.

5. LIFE EXPERIENCE. This is a vibration that Pythagoras probably did not fully understand and one of which modern interpreters have very little to say.

It is plainly the expansion or extension of number 1 and the point of the cycle of reaction at which a new receptivity to life or energy is born. It indicates personal liberty, the opportunity to take a new grasp upon life. It is recreative rather than creative. It is unable to regulate its interest in life and living and its desire to experience sensation. Attracted by everything, held by nothing. Inspiration. Optimism. Variety. Vision. Ease. Fascination. Companionship. Reliance on the principle of life rather than on the immediate expression of which it is often unconscious.

A 5 person often starts things but seldom finishes them, and with a 3 or 9 in conjunction encourages a great deal of advertisement; many plans are made that often come to naught. The unexpected usually proves to be productive of the best results for this vibration, and 5 people usually do well to act upon inspiration. To make extensive preparation, and desire too earnestly for results, is nearly always certain to bring dissatisfaction.

6. COSMIC ADJUSTMENT. This vibration gives the love of home and friends, and means respectability, and domesticity. These people make loyal and substantial friends, and are very reliable expressions. They like to feel that they are trusted by those above them, and have a tendency to undertake responsibility and much work for others. They are naturally the helpers and comforters of the race, and being conscientious, finish whatever they undertake even at some personal inconvenience rather than relinquish anything before it is finished. They work for work's sake and not for material gain, and are more happy when actively engaged than in any

position where they have to learn to "kill time."

Their attraction for money is more settled than the 5 and their ability to accumulate is stronger.

A 6 person is thorough in execution, but is a poor advertiser. He knows intuitively his own possibilities and how a certain thing will result, without being able to explain the details beforehand.

The desire to attach themselves to other expressions is strong, and a 6 individual often satisfies this desire by taking on domesticity, or becoming invaluable to another life in positions of responsibility.

This is the vibration of home and children, where marriage is dictated by the love of home and respectability. There are many unmarried persons in this vibration, of course, but they are cosmic guardians always, taking their lesson indirectly by looking after other people's responsibilities, their relatives, or in caring for pets. This vibration leads to conservatism and upholds respectability, morality, honesty, home and country. It has not much tolerance for people who through the nature of different vibrations are taking their experiences in zones where these standards are absent.

7. SUBJECTIVE DEVELOPMENT. The vibration of the finished worker. Rest. Alone-

ness. Reflection. Worship. In this vibration persons work more because they have to than because they like it. It is very usual to hear a 7 remark, "I have finished my work," without realizing that they are voicing a truth which their vibration stands for. The temple atmosphere, giving a tendency to maintain a "shrine" around the life. Attraction to dim lights and soft colors and to be rather jealous of personal affairs.

A vibration always misrepresented because so little in accord with material law, and somewhat illogical.

It is not what a 7 expresses, but what it does not express, that is the true indication of its character, and it is only when among a circle of friends that it has any possibility of expressing in the way it wishes to, and of showing the beauty and depth of its own inclusion.

At other times, out in the world among strangers, 7 is self-conscious, awkward, desiring to express, but remaining silent because of past experience that expressions may prove unwelcome.

7 people do not invite personal inquiries, and while they often are sympathetic, affable and very good listeners, are not inclined to talk about themselves or their own private affairs. They are more inclined to take these with them in their silence, since they are given very much to re-arrangement of their life in thought, and like

nothing better than to get away with nature and decide for themselves the perplexing problems of their lives.

8. MATERIAL FREEDOM. This vibration is the composite of 2, 4 and 8 and has the vibrations of these numbers included, which gives it supremacy upon the material plane.

8 and 9 show freedom in two distinct zones and being the first of this series of numbers, its influence is most strongly seen to affect the intellectual plane and to bring about material benefits.

An 8 is able and competent to solve all material problems. His judgment is sound in business matters and in the final settlement of ways and means. The employer's consciousness.

This number gives happiness only in positions where material freedom is present, but its attraction is such that wealth and supply will always come when needed to supply an actual want.

An 8 strives for honor, name, place and power, and does all he can to attain this. Unlike the 4, he often gains reward and recognition for his efforts, since he is able to pass the proofs of his material mastership.

This vibration is the realization of the 2 and the 4 and is the fulfillment of their less inspirational experiences.

There is always a seeking in this vibration for proof of spiritual things, although 8's seldom find what they are seeking, or are able to combine the spiritual with the material to their satisfaction. Many spiritists are recruited from this number because having to see before they can believe, the possibility of "materialization" is attractive to them.

9. COMPLETION. Corresponding to the second free number and vibrating to the soul or intuitional, this number gives deeper human initiation and understanding.

Its influence is emotional, passionate and extreme; its expression is governed by the heart rather than by the head.

Since 9 is three times three, the developed 9 has the gifts of the 3 three times included. This inclusion tends to make this vibration very powerful and almost ponderous in expression. The 9 will take on many things that require too much effort for the ordinary person to accomplish. This is why, although they intend to fulfill all promises, material interferences on which they did not reckon are likely to prevent them from doing so.

They cannot be tied down to small conditions or orthodoxy, since, moving in a big orbit or zone of consciousness, they demand freedom in action and thought. This freedom that they demand for themselves they demand for others. They do not admit the right of one individual to coerce and control the actions of another, and they are often led by their intense sympathy to rebel against law and order.

They do not care for possessions or to use their time in accumulating them, but since this vibration has a wonderful power of attraction, what they seek seeks them.

Like the 3, 9 desires to express, but more universally. It usually prefers the pen to the spoken word, unless it chooses to express through art, in music, in painting, in drama, or tragedy, being more addicted to the stage than to the pulpit.

Since 9 is given in Pythagoras' Law of Opposites as "good and evil," the world often tempts one having this number. In order to get the highest good from this vibration, persons having it should be true to their ideals at all times, for, if this is not done, personal desire will claim the life, and remorse and unrest is manifest in the environment.

In the conjunction of 3, 6 and 9, we have the perfect trinity of artistic expression, and like the 3 and 5, 9's are often only really reliable when there are chances for advancement, being naturally ambitious. In this, as in all other odd vibrations, anticipation is more attractive than attainment and possession.

SPECIAL VIBRATIONS OF 11 AND 22.

Mrs. L. Dow Balliett, a teacher of the modern world who has given many revelations and will be recognized as the founder of the Balliett Philosophy of Number Vibration, gives great importance to the numbers 11 and 22 as explaining a further evolution of man after the nine human vibrations have been passed. In practice, the author finds that these numbers really explain those individuals who show in their expression a little more idealism than could perhaps be drawn from the cycle of 1 to 9 in its relation to character.

Numerology seems to show that wherever these vibrations appear they indicate the possibility of spirituality and co-operation, respectively, but not necessarily the expression of these principles. These numbers can always be considered specially wherever found, but where 11 is discovered in the ordinary individual of little education it is seldom more than a little higher phase of 2 and differs, if at all, from the ordinary 2 in the fact that the psychical faculties can be appealed to by those who understand the law of vibration.

Those who have worked among the masses will realize the application of this principle for they will have found one individual here and there, not at all developed in expression, yet quite eager to listen intelligently to higher ideas, which the group of his fellows in the same position in life will not tolerate.

The fact that names vibrating to these numbers of 11 and 22 are often found to be minus many of the numbers in the cycle of 1 to 9 which is necessary to the complete human character, would seem logically to exclude the belief that their presence indicates perfection. The author has repeated his explanations of these two numbers which were given in former editions of "Numerology" so that the many number students who believe that 11 and 22 should not be added may find other angles from which to regard them. In Chapter V is given an example of the author's method by which these two numbers are taken into account in the delineation of character without interrupting the individual's place in the Universal scheme of vibration which has already been shown to be based upon the structure of 1 to 9.

11. REVELATION. It will be seen that 11 is a 2 made up of two 1's. Therefore, the 11 vibration when it is realized can be said to be individualized and doubly creative.

Number 11 does not give ability to direct and control in the practical, physical and commercial fields, but it attracts responsibility of a more artistic character through its impulse to do big inspirational things and to express as a teacher and inspirer of humanity. This number gives dissatisfaction with anything but the development of the highest and the best in the surroundings. The general aspect is readily understood to be genial, affable, refined, inquisitive, in a more individualized way, than the quieter 2 vibration. Able to elevate and inspire surroundings and associates by purity of example and expression of idealism.

22. MASTERSHIP. This vibration is always found to be more adaptable to practical, physical and intellectual expression than the 11, because there is a conjunction of physical energy and material force that enables it to bring its message and idealism more within the comprehension of the masses.

This is a master vibration because master as a word, vibrates 22 and also because the conception of mastership is the ability to be unlimited in understanding and expression. However developed, 22 gives the ability to take a message to "the King in his Palace" and to the road maker with equal assurance that he will be understood.

22 is the number of illustration and encourages varied methods of illustrating an idea in order to make the meaning clear to a mind that cannot follow flights of fancy or rhetorical delivery. It can really demonstrate practically the fundamental principles of truth.

22 is able to do as well as talk and enthuse, and it is often found expressing through actual intellectual and physical interests.

The purpose of this vibration is to elevate the physical to the plane of the psychical, and that is the reason why 22 is the number of many successful inventors of mechanical improvements.

Lesson One of The Cheasley Home Study Course.

CHAPTER III

CONSTRUCTIVE AND DESTRUCTIVE ASPECTS

The individual who is living to the constructive development of his character numbers is on the path of destiny, while he who answers to the destructive is building for the future "karmic" or fatal effects which will result sometime in his expression in the Negative aspect of limitation.

Those who come into this knowledge may profit by it; and by the knowledge of their own vibrations and the comparison of their every-day expression of them with what is given as Constructive and Destructive in this chapter, can adjust themselves constructively in Universal harmony. It is usual to find construction in some principles and destruction in others.

Bear in mind that there are no higher or lower vibrations, neither is one better than another; each is distinct in its own orbit, although 1 is the slowest and 9 is the most vibrant, or fastest. The standards of one must never be compared with another since each is governed by its own law, although necessary to its neighbor.

1. The constructive expression — INDIVIDUALIZATION, conscious of its own importance, but not blind to the rights of others or inconsiderate of their opinions. Asks the advice of others, but uses this advice only as an aid to its own opinion which is and should be dictated by the feeling of confidence in its own expressions. Chooses freely from the expressions around it the things it needs for a more perfect expression of its individuality, does not hang on to any expression too long but discards readily the things it has outgrown in order that it may pass on to higher and more developed opportunities. Loves and gives without thought of personal gain and makes willing unity with all conditions without resistance or self-pity for the expressions it is called on to surrender.

The Destructive expression — DOMINANT. Egotistical, inconsiderate of other people's opinion and always attempting to live other people's lives for them instead of minding its own business. Seeks to hold things and individuals to its own personal life and surrenders individuals only with resistance.

Gives advice where it is not asked; has only one method and that its own; is not given to study the feelings of other people if it takes a fancy to attain; and is "I," "I," "I" all through life.

2. The constructive expression — DIPLOMACY, PLIABILITY, tactful, anxious to please. Never aggressive, but rather waiting for the opinion of the other person before expressing its own opinions too forcibly. Willing to learn and collect all the knowledge on all subjects and to mix freely and on a basis of equality, with its fellow beings. Willing to learn by performing the smallest service. Puts itself under the law of receiving and serving. Will make any effort for peace and will seek to appease the anger of others by keeping its own temper.

It is individualized but its individuality gained in the initiation of the 1, is kept in the background and is only expressed in a positive, persistent way and never dominantly.

The destructive expression — INDIFFERENCE, rather disgruntled, easily roused to anger when it becomes wilfully destructive, tearing down instead of building up by patience and persistence as the constructive expression does. Not caring to mix, and having no great development of individuality, lacks pride in its personal expressions and is often careless in all directions, abiding only by the standards it sets for itself.

Makes all kinds of promises but seldom fulfills any of them because it dislikes being brought to account or forced to a decision. Deceptive. Indulgent. Degenerate.

3. The Construction expression—AMBITION. Takes every opportunity offered for self-expression and seeks to become more accomplished that it may make the most of future opportunities for its own and others' advancement. Is sociable, always willing to entertain without making itself a nuisance. Strives to be the last word in the expression of personality, through good clothes, artistic arrangement in the surroundings and the development of individual talent as a life's work. Inspirational, not seeking work with the hands but rather in the inspirational, professional, artistic zones. Strives to become the welcome and interesting companion, to be as concentrated in its interests as possible, always tolerant of other people's errors and awake to its own. Expresses patience in waiting for the materialization of its own creations and tolerance in dealing with the effects of others.

The destructive expressions—I N T O L E RANCE. Selfish; not a very high principle; taking every means as legitimate in order to get the things it needs for personal expression. Not serious enough to perfect itself in any accomplishment fully, but following the latest fashions in everything, very unconcentrated, not really knowing what it wants for any length of time. Very exacting and critical, engaged in endless competition with others for the highest expression of self and never really contented. Impatient; feather-brained; self-sufficient.

4. The constructive expression—S T E A D-FASTNESS. Governed by the intellect, paying close attention to detail work in life, but seeking to raise itself by a higher perfection in technicality so that it may have freedom in the material zone. Ambitious to rise to a place of power in the material side of life, willing to study and work hard to achieve its end in the meanwhile, contented with its progress. Not interested in spiritual or intuitional expressions that cannot be proved by facts, or in rebellion against legimate control or the expression of service in its own life. Very honest, reliable, exact. Practical and can obey orders.

The destructive expression—DISCONTENT. Dissatisfied with service. Always considers that it is being exploited by the employer. Clock watchers and servants only because they have to live somehow. Aspire to the high places of control without trying to prepare themselves for them. "As good as everybody else" in their own estimation, and always causing trouble in the labor fields by inciting their fellows to use force to resist authority and to assert their equality. Crude. Vulgar. Physical in their tastes. Ill-mannered.

5. The constructive expression—NEW LIFE. Inspirational, intuitional and inventive, personally free, a traveller, a welcome companion, meets life with open arms ready to make unity with every experience that it meets as a means for higher unfoldment and expansion of the self. Endeavors to attain a Christ-like expression by its universality and versatility, yet knows what it wants without needing to plan and prepare for its goal. Relies upon the unexpected rather than anticipating results and through faith and confidence in its own quality of expression is optimistic, fascinating, a booster, expressing sympathy with other people's troubles and courage in its own.

Lives close to its ideals and develops something in its life along scientific lines that occupies its time and yet provides it with new interest continually.

The destructive expression—INDULGENCE. Expresses through self-indulgence in sex, appetite and self. Is very uncertain in its vibration, being rather changeable in its actions. Rather poor moral standard and yet carries off its actions with a good deal of bravado which disarms many who would otherwise condemn.

Procrastinates; is not a very good investment as an employee or as a friend, since it cannot be depended upon to make good although it is always full of ideas that gain people's confidence. They resist change in the things of their own personal life and destroy their opportunities by holding on too long to things in a manner similar to the 1 vibration, desiring for selfish results.

6. The Constructive. RELIABILITY. The comforter. The willing helper, conscientious. Maintains its individuality even in serving. Has great love of home, relatives and friends, and never wishes to live alone or for the self alone. Always expressing cheerfulness, never despondent, always the busy finisher of what it undertakes, satisfied with pleasures of a quiet nature, a restful, soothing, modest, influence.

The Destructive — INTERFERENCE. Too anxious to serve even where not asked. Overburdens itself with the things it voluntarily takes on to do for others. Is not such a restful influence since it is always anxious and bustling, and cannot take ordered time for rest. Refuses to believe that anyone else can do anything so well or so thoroughly as itself, and is constantly too free with advice and well meant suggestion.

7. The Constructive — PLACIDITY. Calm. Refined. Studious. Not seeking for expression in objective things but asking only the opportunity to give something to the world that can reveal the beauty of deeper truth. Not seeking

to control business or finance, but content to be left alone to develop something in its own life that can attract supply to it.

7 people engage in work that takes them away from the bustle and confusion of commerce where they can give their revelation from "behind the scenes" as it were.

While often living their lives alone the 7 people are never lonely, for through their inner development, their worship and introspection, they see a world of beauty and companionship hidden from the average sight and feeling. They do not condemn expressions with which they cannot harmonize, but contact life without prejudice, and with their faith centered in the underlying principles of life, are enabled to rise superior to outward difficulties. This vibration means secrecy and conservation of energy; it makes a good listener and knows how to make every experience provide it with food for thought and deeper development.

The Destructive—TURBULENCE. Rather difficult people to live with since they are individualized and endeavor to make other people conform to their rather peculiar methods of expression. Condemn the things they cannot understand; imagine themselves possessed of ability in practical and commercial lines, and seek to direct and control in these directions, only to be frustrated by superior intelligences. Unreasonable. Obstinate. Autocratic. Endeavor to force quiet in their surroundings by restraining other people from natural expression.

8. The Constructive—JUSTICE. Successful in commercial expressions. Directors, organizers, employers, industrial heads, mathematicians and master manipulators of physical values. Take a personal interest, as far as possible, in those around them, in employees or assistants, and while using the efforts of these individuals legitimately to build their own success, endeavor at the same time to give them opportunities for perfection and advancement. Very even-tempered individuals, with a good balance of reason and intuition, but inclined to be led by the former. Upholders of fair dealing. Masters of their emotional impulses and physical reactions.

The Destructive—INJUSTICE. Successful in direction and management but destructive in their use of power, sweating those under them and taking the role of the oppressor and "boss." They seek to keep every other person subject to their personality and will and never co-operate, only command. Are unscrupulous in their efforts to obtain and maintain their physical and intellectual superiority. Their main ideal in life is money because of the control this can afford them, and they judge every opportunity and association by the material advantage to themselves.

9. The constructive expression—LOVE. Humanitarians, philanthrophists, regarding all people of whatever race, color or creed as brothers. Have the highest expression of *impersonal* love, sending out in their contact with others, only love, justice, mercy, seeking to make every man their friend. Exercising the power of healing consciously or unconsciously, by speaking the right word at the right time and helping people in their troubles. Rely more on their intuitional faculty than on the intellectual, and realizing their power over all other human expressions seek only to use their influence constructively. Stand as revelators through art, through the power of healing or as counsellors, and are giving willing service to humanity. They have learned to transmute all passion into love and all personal desire into universal understanding; free to go where they will, welcomed by everyone, princes of earthly expression.

The destructive expression—DESIRE. Rather personal in their expressions and desires. Make distinctions between human beings extending far past their ordinary expressions. Use destructively to gain their own ends and for their own self satisfaction, the power they have over those around them, by taking advantage of people's confidence, in business, love or friendship. They play on the emotions of their own and other's compositions like a harpist on his instrument, expressing in anger, violent blasting passion, and personal love, and raising these emotions in others at will. In this expression, they use the power of dramatic speech and emotional expression destructively, and know how to wound by their words as no other vibration does, biting in their sarcasm, aggravating and passionate.

This is the most destructive expression even according to Universal standards, for in this vibration homes are laid desolate, hearts broken, trust betrayed and the individual's life surrounded with dead ashes of memory and physical wastes of disease.

11. The constructive expression—IDEALISM. Individualized, serene and equalized, ready to make unity with all people and conditions, but maintaining their own individuality always and their self respect. Endeavoring to make their life expressions the means of a revelation of high spiritual truth and usefulness by things they do and say; engaged in uplifting and helping others. Taking thought only of the ideal and spiritual truth of the things in which they are engaged. Demanding the best and highest from themselves and others, but never unreasonable or blind to the shortcomings of the human plane.

The destructive expression—ANTAGONISM.

Agnostics. Ridicule the good in everything, are not interested in spiritual truths. Domineering, exacting, and extremely critical and disparaging of other people's expressions. Mercenary and attempt to control commercial expressions rather than to rest on the elevation of something high in their own life which can attract to them the things they desire.

22. The constructive expression—CO-OPERATION. Calm, expressing power and poise in outward expressions and having these principles well included. Are practical and thorough to a degree, and expressing the principle of co-operation in all their dealings with others. Draw all men unto them for some great Universal purpose of good, fulfill the expectations of the many that believe in them, by using the highest and most powerful effort to fulfill their trust. Organizers, promoters of co-operative movements in the commercial, religious and political world. Striving always to make their own expression the combination of spirituality and materiality by expressing a high ideal through practical and understandable methods.

The destructive expression—UNRELIABLE. Full of great ideas of co-operation but too indolent to carry them out. Betray people's confidence by falling short of their advertised ultimate. Bogus company promoters, floating one after another of their wonderful but impossible ideas. Very similar to the destructive 9 in other characteristics but not so emotional or extreme.

Lesson Two of The Cheasley Home Study Course.

CHAPTER IV

NEGATIVE ASPECTS

As the explanations given below are followed it will not be difficult to discover the expressions of many individuals one meets in a day's living.

The man who shines your shoes, the woman who scrubs your floors, may both be above the plane on which they are living, possessed of powerful vibrations apparent to us through their personality, but to them as yet unknown or undiscovered in this incarnation, waiting for the circumstance or individual to speak them into freedom and new creation.

Again, the artist born into inartistic families, the individuals entitled by the strength of their vibrations to material freedom, living in a home where to get every meal is a struggle; all these expressions and more are explained by the laws of vibration, and are given in the aspect of Negativity the opportunity to work back again into birthrights they forfeited sometime, somewhere.

As you follow the negative characteristics it will be easy to relate in your mind the three aspects of the numbers if the example given in the foregoing paragraphs is remembered.

NUMEROLOGY

NEGATIVE ASPECTS

1. LIMITATION. Individuals with little backbone in life even though their Expression is 1. Often seen as those people who could do higher work in life if they could only be raised to a consciousness of themselves. Victims of their own destructive law in the past, these individuals are often seen as blind, deaf or afflicted in some way, where they have never had an opportunity in this life to assert individuality or to be self-reliant, but have always been dependent on others.

2. INDECISION. Lacks the force to gain very much for itself. Has very few individual opinions and readily reflects the ideas and expressions of people around it. Is too easily persuaded into doing meaner work for other people; is seldom contented but feels the burden of life and living rather heavily. While it is not disgruntled, does not feel the urge to mix with others.

3. REPRESSION. Will not or cannot take advantage of opportunities offered to express the self, in artistic or any other lines. Unconcentrated; undecided, cannot make up their mind to any one expression but taking up many things, doing a little of one and a little of another. Victims of their own destructive law in the past, are seen with the desire to express, but in an environ-

ment where accomplishment and higher development is impossible to them; led by circumstances to engage in unsuitable technical work.

4. LACK OF AMBITION. Just mechanical workers, working because they have to live and not for their personal advancement in any way. Not a very high development of intellect, asking only the opportunity to work and live from day to day. Work, sleep and eat.

5. CRUCIFIXION. Always seen to be fighting some little "fox in the vines" or some subtle craving for self-indulgence above which it is hard to rise. Has a good deal of surrender of the things it values most many times because of the little indulgences it lacks the strength in itself to overcome. Financial loss and negation to include. These individuals are often pictures of their destructive self-indulgence of the past, through devitalized bodies, disease and deformity.

6. ANXIETY. Overburdened by the care of homes, indiivduals and institutions; imposed upon by relatives. Ill at ease outside of their particular country, home or business. Are over-anxious for those dependent upon them for attention and inclined to become anchored to some stronger individual whose thoughts and actions it copies to the detriment of its own development. Rather depressing; tired through service.

7. FEAR. Unable to express anything that they feel in the inner nature; consider that no one wants them or understands them or that they ever had a chance. Victims of destructive laws in the past, this vibration is surrounded with many responsibilities and relations from which they find it hard to be free. It prevents them from gaining the opportunity to be alone which is so necessary to their growth. Filled with fear over the possibility of failure and loneliness in the future; easily disturbed by outward appearances which they accept as realities.

8. FAILURE. Unsuccessful in speculation and investment. Find it difficult to gain the prestige they feel belongs to them in the business world. Victims of the destructive laws of the past, are seen to be born into a family and to live in an environment where there is lack of material freedom instead of constant opportunity; where money is scarce and where they have to give the meaner expressions of service.

9. EMOTION. Full of contradictory vibrations; too easily moved by the things that appeal to the emotional nature. Undermine their expression by being over-generous and take the troubles of others to themselves, weeping with those that weep, giving to all that ask, even beggaring themselves. Have lost the power of using other people either for good or bad, and are im-

posed upon by others freely. Unable to obtain much for themselves as they are torn this way and that by the force of their own emotions.

11. UNDEVELOPMENT. Often doing menial work in life. Victims of their own destructive law in the past, are seen in environments with little chance of spiritual development and where they remain ignorant of the idealistic characteristics of their vibration. Despondent. Ineffectual.

22. UNDEVELOPMENT. Doing just ordinary work in the commercial world, having a good deal of service and little development of their power for organization and co-operation. As the victims of their destructive law of the past, are often seen with weak bodies entirely unsuited to be the vehicles of any idealized expression they may wish to develop. Invalids that lack the physical strength to accomplish their high ideas.

In the negative expressions of the 11 and 22 are often seen those who are insane; the 11's often with religious mania although they may not to people's knowledge have been religious at all when in their right mind and the 22's with misconceived ideas of their positions in life and an illogical expression that is nothing but a travesty on their constructive possibilities.

Lesson Three of The Cheasley Home Study Course.

CHAPTER V

WHAT THE NAME MEANS

"What's in a name?" is an expression that we often hear spoken carelessly, without being able to supply a convincing answer. It is this answer that NUMEROLOGY supplies by interpreting the true characteristics in the expression of everything that lays claim to possess a name which is its own and by which it is recognized among men.

In the name of anything we have simply the vowels and consonants from which to adjudge its vibrations.

Mrs. L. Dow Balliett was apparently the first teacher to discover the value of the vowels, which she uses to show the spirit force of every expression in the same way that the vowels are the voice of a language.

The value of the consonants, the shell of a language, was first discovered by Dr. Julia Seton, founder of the New Thought Church and School (Church of the New Civilization), who recognizes that the consonants decide the personality of the individual or thing under consideration.

NUMEROLOGY dealing with individuals in

character analyzation, deals with the baptismal name; that is, all the christian names and surnames you received at baptism, or if you were not baptised, those given by your parents or guardians. It interprets the character from three distinct standpoints called respectively: IDEALITY, IMPRESSION and EXPRESSION.

The vibration of the first is found from the simple addition of all the vowels in your name, the second is found from the addition of all the consonants, and the third and last, from the addition of both the vowels and consonants.

"Addition" does not mean the adding up of the number of vowels, and consonants that appear, but in adding the numbers that appear under each letter of your name after you have conformed to the following rules given in, "Casting the name for analysis."

First however, it is necessary to understand fully the meaning of the terms IDEALITY, IMPRESSION and EXPRESSION.

It is understood that there is often a great difference between what an individual desires to do; his personality or appearance; and the methods by which he may actually express himself in relation to his opportunities. This difference is revealed in every individual by a comparison of Ideality, Impression and Expression.

The Ideality number tells the character of the desire nature, of the ambitions, the real conceptions of life, the quality of the urge which must vitalize each thought and action, the true inner force and worth of everything that exists.

The Impression is the most objective division of the character although not unimportant, because no matter how great or developed the Ideality number may be, it can be hidden from the world at large by a weaker Impression. It tells the characteristics observed on first acquaintance, the impression given by the personal appearance before there is any speech or action—what we look like.

The Expression tells our place in the scheme of things; as we express in the form of the thinking, acting conscious individual. It reveals the thing for which we have the greatest aptitude as well as the characteristic we utilize in the most trivial actions in which we engage.

These three divisions of the character can be memorized as Ideality—Desire, Impression—Appearance, Expression—General Ability.

Our name is an exact record of our place in the cosmic plan; it is not an accident but a vibratory structure that we have built somewhere, have created, experienced and are now come to express. It tells our inclusion in the law of human experience and is the effect of causes put in motion since we first entered the human consciousness, just as the Path of Life (Chapter seven) of the present life, indicates the causes we are meeting in this incarnation.

CASTING THE NAME FOR ANALYSIS. The following is the plan of Pythagoras' vibratory cycle of 1 to 9 with the alphabet arranged in three divisions.

```
1  2  3  4  5  6  7  8  9
A  B  C  D  E  F  G  H  I
J  K  L  M  N  O  P  Q  R
S  T  U  V  W  X  Y  Z
```

The following example of preparing a name is the clearest known method and will afford the utmost ease in reading any name if each detail is followed as given.

$$
\begin{array}{ll}
1 + 1=2 \text{ IDEALITY} \\
1+   1+0 \\
9 \;+\; 1 = 10 1 \;+\; 9 \;=\; 10 \\
\text{R I C H A R D} \text{H A R D I N G} \\
9+\;3+8\;+\;9+4{=}33 8+9+4+5+7{=}33 \\
3+3   3+3 \\
6   + 6{=}12 \\
 1+2 = 3 = \text{IMPRESSION}
\end{array}
$$

R I C H A R D   H A R D I N G
9+9+3+8+1+9+4=43   8+1+9+4+9+5+7=43
     4+3   4+3
      7   +   7 = 14
             1+4   = 5 Expression

In this example we have first dealt with the vowels, placing over the top of each, the number that corresponds to it in the table given. We have added together the numbers thus given until we have obtained a single digit, which has given us the Ideality.

The Ideality we have seen tells the basis of the character, the real strength of our inner ideals and desires; what we really are, as distinct from anything that we may appear to be. When a person's every-day expression for instance, is interrupted by adverse circumstances, the vibration relied upon for new inspiration to rise, is that of the Ideality. It depends therefore on this vibration, whether the individual is really ambitious, religious, material, inspirational in the heart of his composition, and when we see any individual doing a big work in life, it tells us just how true this expression is to the real ideal of the individual or the motive that prompts its continuance.

When the Ideality has been found, turn to its number in Chapters Two and Three, remembering always that dealing with the Ideality, the explanations given will correspond to the inner ideals or what it is desired to express.

Referring again to the name we have cast, we see that the consonants were the next to be dealt with, and that dealing with each name separately, we found at last a final digit, 3, which told us the Impression. Turning to the explanations of the numbers again will tell the characteristics which it would appear that this individual possessed.

A final reference to the second casting of the name shows that both the vowels and the consonants are added together until the final digit of 5 is obtained.

Reference to No. 5 in our Explanations (Chapters II and III) will tell what this individual really expresses in every-day life.

THE RULE OF 11 AND 22

When either of these numbers is found as the digit of a single name they can be allowed to stand as found and not added in with any other numbers or digits until the final total of all the names is being made. The following is an example:

V I O L E T
4+9+6+3+5+2=29 = 11

V I C T O R I A
4+9+3+2+6+9+9+1=43 = 7

B U R G E S S
2+3+9+7+5+1+1=28 = 1

| 1st Name | | 2d Name | | 3d Name |
| 11 | + | 7 | + | 10 |

11-8=19=10=(1)=Expression

By treating the 11 found as the digit of Violet as an ordinary number we would have disclosed a final digit of 1 by the arrangement of 11+7+1 =19=1+9=10 (cross off cipher)=1.

We obtained instead, 11-8 which is called a "combination 1" because its creative force is definitely obtained by the combination of idealism =11 and material freedom=8 in daily expression, and is not an abstract creative ability as an ordinary 1 would be, capable of development by individualization, the constructive principle of 1.

The law governing the interpretation of all combination numbers is simple whether the combination is made by 11 or 22.

11 we have learned stands for Revelation, and the number that is in combination with it determines the zone through or to which this revelation should be expressed. 11-8 then is a revelation through the expression of the 8 vibration—business, commerce, material and intellectual freedom; and the creative principle coming from the addition of the 11 to the 8 (11+8=19=10=1) should be made by this a more specialized development. 11-9 means revelation through Art, Emotion and complete expression and all that the 9 stands for; and to accomplish this would be to express the association and experience of the 2 vibration.

What is meant by the term "Revelation?" Taking a message of higher truth to, and developing the most ideal standard in all relationships.

22 stands for the perfect balance between high ideals and practical methods, so that where 22 is found as the dominating force in any combination number, it reveals that it is the constructive expression of the individual to stand for a co-operative force in the zone determined by the ordinary number that makes such combination.

It will be readily understood that the higher possibilities of the 11 and 22 are not easy for any individual to realize without constant attention to the constructive side of every expression no matter how small; and where the higher freedom of the combinations of 11 and 22 has not been realized or attempted, it is interesting to note that the expression conforms always to the ordinary final digit. 11-8 Expression unawakened would conform to 1; 11-9 to 2, 22-8 to 4 and so on.

Lesson Four of The Cheasley Home Study Course.

CHAPTER VI

NAMES DIGITS—EACH NUMBER—SURNAMES

In the understanding of what can be ascertained by the casting of our number-scope, it is important to bear in mind that our full baptismal name is the true record of the inclusion of past initiations, the plan of vibration that determines what we are qualified to express in this life and a statement of the materials we have at our disposal with which to build our house of living. A knowledge of vibration can tell us quickly the forces we lack and those in which we are included.

We shall find it interesting then, while regarding the numbers of the IDEALITY, IMPRESSION and EXPRESSION that we have already dealt with as the most important, to consider briefly each number under each letter of each of our names, for from this effort we shall learn many things that NUMEROLOGY as the scientific number study regards as helpful to the perfect delineation of individual character and ability.

Each number under each letter of the name is a distinct vibration, which although tempered by its neighbors, since it is only a part of the whole force, is nevertheless accountable for some part of the individual's every-day Expression.

Even numbers, as we have already seen, show inclusion or understanding on the material, intellectual planes, odd numbers show inclusion and understanding on the spiritual and intuitional; so that it is necessary only to find in which zone we have the greater inclusion, in order to determine where our true ability in life lies.

This theory carried into practice generally, does much to determine which individuals of those around us can be trusted in matters of finance or to conform to plain material standards when given material responsibilities; likewise those who can be trusted in positions where inspiration, initiative, artistic or creative ability is necessary.

"Honesty" and "Dishonesty" are nothing but the attention to or the violation of this law in vibration, for "dishonesty" is not only expressed in material things, as generally accepted, but is engendered wherever individuals are attempting to conform to standards of a plane of which they are ignorant, while beside them is the path of hidden possibilities in another and better understood zone.

To illustrate this law we can use the following example:

                                    Ideality.
              2   +   6 = 8
            2+0
       5+1 +   9 + 5=20 1 +   5 = 6
       B E A T R I C E   B A R N E S
       2 5 1 2 9 9 3 5   2 1 9 5 5 1

to check these numbers refer to chart in Chapter
II. Here are found:

                (2 appears 3 times
                (4   nil
                (6   nil
even numbers (8   nil
                (———
                (total 3

               (1 appears 3 times ..
               (3   "   1   "
               (5   "   4   "
odd numbers (7   nil
               (9 appears 3 times
               (———
               (total 11

This individual has the greater number of initiations in the odd numbers, which means that in emergencies and on the intuitional plane generally, where creative ability is shown in thought and act, there will be an unconscious ability expressed; while in the material plane the efforts will be conscious and uncertain of success.

In conjunction with this theory we consider the number of the Ideality, for if this number is opposite the inclusion, as in this instance, 8 being an even number and the inclusion being in the odd zone, it tells that the Ideal is strong enough to force the individual to conform to "honesty" in the zone in which he is not qualified to succeed in the general sense.

If the number of the Ideality agrees with the inclusion, we take it into account only as the indication that there is no opposite ideal to urge conformity to the standards of a plane in which he is not sure of himself and neither has any desire to follow.

The laws are as follows:

Even Inclusion and odd Ideality—capability and honesty in the material. A desire to be honest and exact in the emotional and intuitional.

Even Inclusion and even Ideality—capability and honesty in the material, no ability to conform to honesty in the intuitional.

Odd Inclusion and even Ideality—capability in the intuitional emotional zones. Desire to be honest and exact in the material.

Odd Inclusion and odd Ideality—Capability in the intuitional and emotional. No ability to be honest in the material; should not be trusted with material responsibilities.

NAME DIGITS

The number that we get for each of our names by adding the vowels and consonants is called the name digit. The comparison of these digits will tell us whether or not our name is harmonious in vibration.

Harmony is shown by the digits all appearing in the odd or all in the even zone, inharmony where one will be an odd number and the other or others will be even, or where two will be even and the other or others odd.

For example,—of two individuals whose Expressions are both 6, one by the name digits of 3, 3 and the other by name digits of 1, 1, 4, the former would have the more harmonious name.

Again, individuals who show evenness in expression have one of two principles of vibration, i. e., Harmony in individual name digits, or Name digits that are close together in value.

Those who are erratic, less concentrated and cover much ground in every-day expression, have either inharmony in digits, or names whose digits are far apart in value.

The only exception to this rule is where the name digits are 1, 2, 3 or 3, 6, 9, which are in both cases even and regular in expression.

The following charts will explain the action of both expressions:

```
                       1st name   2d name   3d name
Digits near in value—     3          5         7
         Intuition      Intellect
            11             22
             9              8
             7              6
             5              4      ..
             3              2
                    1
```

```
                       1st name   2d name   3d name
Digits far apart in value—
                          3          8         3
         Intuition      Intellect
            11             22
             9              8
             7              6
             5              4      ..
             3              2
                    1
```

The line shows the course taken in Expression by the two individuals; one with name digits 3, 5, 7, and the other with name digits 3, 8, 1; the first regular and in the same zone, the second erratic by reason of operation in both zones, veering from intuitional emotional to intellectual and practical and almost back again.

The final digit of the whole name—the Expression, with which we have dealt previously as being obtained from the addition of the individual name digits, has the greatest influence of all and determines our real point at the cycle of 1 to 9 vibrations. When Numerologists use the term "a number 2 person," "a number 6 person," etc., it is this Expression number that should be implied.

CHAPTER VII

WHAT THE BIRTH DATE INDICATES

As in Astrology, the date of a person's birth plays an important part in character delineation by Numerology.

The baptismal Name of an individual tells what the soul has included in the past and what it is qualified to express in the present, but the vibrations of the day, month and year of birth, indicate what has next to be included.

The Number gained by the addition of the vibrations of the birth date denotes exactly the initiation which it is to the individual's highest good to include in harmonious adjustment. It undoubtedly constitutes the greatest attracting force of a life, being responsible, as it is, for the conditions among which the person finds himself from time to time. It attracts the cities and countries in which he lives, his companions and positions, and shows clearly the possibility of expressing himself in the way he desires and of attaining his ideals. Whatever forces are shown on the PATH OF LIFE, as the vibrations of birth are called, will have to be met and included whether harmoniously or otherwise, since they constitute the inclusion of certain lessons that the soul wishes to express in a future life.

The method of determining the vibration of the Path of Life is very simple—the calendar number of the month is placed underneath whichever month opens the date of birth; this is followed by the addition of the number of the day and the digit found by adding the numbers in the year, as follows:

```
August    2+8    1+8+9+1—Aug. 28, 1891
   8      1+0      1+9
   8       1       1+0
   8+      1  +    1=10=1 PATH OF LIFE.
```

To aid one to understand better what influence THE PATH OF LIFE will have on the expression of an individual, and whether the life will be easy or difficult, Numerology compares it with the vibration of the EXPRESSION, and whenever we see this duplicated as the digit of the PATH OF LIFE, we may know that the individual will have little to contend with in life; for instance, an EXPRESSION 4, on a PATH OF LIFE vibrating 4, would not be expected to meet anything not easily overcome, since although it might meet some conflicting influences under the separate vibrations of the month, day and year of the birth date, it is strongly connected through life with its own force.

This is the path of Self-perfection where the soul has the opportunity to round off, as it were, the inclusion of a former lesson.

There are many individuals found with a PATH OF LIFE weaker in vibration than their EXPRESSION, and these people are always connected with expressions of life and people who are beneath them. Whatever they attain is the result of their own efforts and not of opportunities and privileges they meet in life. Their complaint is that they are withheld from the opportunities their soul desires; if they did but realize it, there is no force in their life strong enough to withhold them from anything. They meet nothing stronger than themselves and are always prepared for emergencies.

This is the path of the Teacher, Revelator and Messenger, rather than that of the student, and is the opportunity the soul takes to express authority.

Lastly, there is the individual whose PATH OF LIFE is found to be higher than the vibration of the EXPRESSION, and this life is always climbing to make itself equal to the many splendid opportunities it meets. This is the most difficult of the three, for the individual must always hug his ideals close to his heart and take care that there are no false steps. It is the path of experience, and gives influential friends, positions and opportunities.

This PATH OF LIFE is the indication that the soul has been true in the past, and as a reward, is given in the present new worlds to conquer.

The golden rule for the harmonious inclusion of the lesson of the PATH OF LIFE is *adjustment;* and in order to help us apply this law, we should understand that it is the purpose of every individual only to intensify the constructive characteristics of the Path of Life.

The essence of the lesson of each vibration with the corresponding "watchwords" which, if held constantly in the mind when faced with difficulty and doubt, can attract success are:

Path of Life	Purpose of Life	Watchword
1	Creation	UNITY
2	Collection	SERVICE
3	Self Expression	PATIENCE
4	Material Production	SERVICE
5	Life Experience	UNITY
6	Adjustment	LOVE (Related)
7	Subjective Development	PEACE
8	Material Perfection	SERVICE
9	Complete Expression	LOVE (impersonal)

11	Revelation	UNITY
22	Co-Operation	PEACE

If the reader will identify his Path of Life number in this chart he will learn the constructive development together with the "watchword" that will promote this to the end of his life: thus he will overcome many obstacles.

READING THE PATH OF LIFE

In reading the Path of Life from the birth date, take first the final digit=1 in the example given earlier in this chapter, and understand that this number and everything it means in the Explanations of the numbers (Chapters II and III) is the main lesson and development this life has to include.

Whatever this number may be, it will appear as the Expression number of many of the most important people and localities in our life: those that are looked upon as being the means of much development.

Secondly, deal with each individual number in the Path of Life (the 8 of the month, the 1 of the day and the 1 of the year in our example), and read these separately as distinct but lesser lessons of the Path of Life, as opportunities which the individual will receive and as associates that can be cultivated for more perfect expression and growth, even though these associations may prove more important than harmonious.

Thirdly, realizing that the complete cycle of human experience is represented by the numbers 1 to 9, discover the numbers from this cycle that do not appear as the digit of the month, day and year of birth. For instance; in our ilustration we have 8, 1, 1, therefore Nos. 2, 3, 4, 5, 6, 7 and 9 are absent. By identifying these numbers with their characteristics it can be shown that opportunities for mixing freely with all kinds of conditions=2, for social and inspirational self-expression=3, for hard mental and physical work=4, for constant change and variety in association and occupation=5, for accepting responsibilities through the care of homes, individuals and institutions=6, for living entirely alone, intensifying subjective development=7, for becoming the humanitarian and philanthrophist=9, should be regarded as phases of experience that will take the individual off the track of the true development offered by this incarnation.

Fourthly, find the Purpose of the Life from the table given and the watchword which agrees with this purpose and will help unfold the divine essence of happiness and success.

Lesson Six of The Cheasley Home Study Course.

CHAPTER VIII

CHANGING THE NAME—SIGNATURES—CHOOSING NAMES.

The Name we receive at birth has been proved to be an exact indication to our character and our ability in this life. It has also been seen, however, that this name from the vibratory standpoint does not always relate us in the best possible attitude to the lessons we came to learn as shown from the PATH OF LIFE.

By changing our name therefore, we adjust ourselves more favorably to the experiences we are bound to meet in this life, giving ourselves a better chance of success. It is a revelation sometimes, if we will just glance over the "materials" at our disposal in this life and try to see whether we have used or are using them in a way to enable us to build the finest "house" according to the plan laid out over our PATH OF LIFE.

In choosing a new name for ourselves or in adjusting the one to which we are already entitled, there are several important but simple rules to be considered:

1. To choose a name that in its final digit is along the same zone, either odd or even, as our own name vibrations, i. e., if our own name is numbered upon the odd side choose a signature with an odd Expression.
2. To choose a name that in the individual digits is harmonious. Names that have a final digit made up of odd and even digits are not harmonious, such as $1+6+7=5$, as such an expression has to be put along two lines, odd and even, and there must be a separation of energy.
3. To choose a name that in its final digit is in the same zone, odd or even, as the PATH OF LIFE vibration, since this leads the life to development in the right direction.

The effect of changing the name and of signing a new signature is to bring around us different influences and conditions by intensifying in our life the force which is seen as its Expression.

The use with a capable knowledge of how to change the name, is of great far-reaching result, for it is often seen that in the signature is the explanation of certain conditions that are provoking us.

It is not advisable to advocate the wholesale changing of names for yourself or others, after this knowledge is included, since all life is initiation and the signature intensifying certain experiences undoubtedly gives us certain initiations that cannot be ignorantly interrupted. There is one infallible indication that the signature should be changed and this is when its bearer is dissatisfied with its form, is unhappy under certain conditions and is willing, without knowing what will happen, to allow the signature to be changed. Such an individual is ready to be lifted out into new experiences.

The change of name only very slightly affects our Ideality, is more apparent in the change which it gives to our Impression and most of all is seen to affect our Expression, bringing out in every-day life just the qualities that its vibration stands for: 1. Individuality and self-reliance. 2. Diplomacy and association. 3. Perfected personal Expression. 4. Technicality and attention to little material things. 5. Change and versatility. 6. Responsibilities, care of individuals. 7. Aloneness, Reflection, Misunderstanding in material things. 8. Direction and control, material freedom. 9. Generosity, Emotion, Art. 11. Idealism, Unity with many conditions. 22. Co-operation, Invention, Practical Expression of Ideals.

SIGNATURES

The signature of a stranger, on a letter or elsewhere, can tell us quickly the characteristics that the individual is intensifying and the vibration through which he is attempting to gain a higher unfoldment for himself. Although we can never really read the inner nature from the Expression of the signature, we have been able to decide very accurately the desire which prompted the intensification of such a vibration. The signature not giving an individual a new Ideality, nevertheless has an Ideality of its own which is told from the vowels of its vibration when this is spelled out, as in the next chapter; and from this Ideality we can tell very clearly for this and other purposes, the real hidden value of each Expression which an individual will show to the world, and the almost unconscious desire which prompted the Expression of the signature digit.

Consideration of the signature of a married woman determines the initiation under which her marriage has placed her life and will be found to explain the new experiences which have been included since its adoption.

The individual who will get the most accurate reading of the signature is the one who is given to intensify one way of signing the name, for where so many different signatures are used, the conditions of the life are more subject to change and less easy to determine as distinct initiations.

CHOOSING NAMES FOR CHILDREN

Naturally such a knowledge of vibration as NUMEROLOGY provides, will lead us to the question of how to name our children, and in this extension there are some very interesting and definite findings.

Numerology does not advocate the choosing of the name of a child by a person outside of the parents, because it looks upon the consciousness of the child as simply an extension of the consciousness of its father and mother. Therefore, it believes that with the parents should rest the choice of a name and that this choice should be made according to harmony in sound. Tone is a much finer scheme of vibration than numbers, and if the sound of a name is harmonious to the parents of a child, that child is invariably found to possess in after life the characteristics of its parents, but in different relationship, and stands revealed to the one who understands human vibration, as a correct extension of the consciousness that attracted it.

When a child's name has been chosen in this way, one who understands the law can step in and by his knowledge explain along what lines the child should be developed, forecasting the experiences that it will meet.

This method of naming children is not endorsed in any other system so far as known, because most teachers prefer to demonstrate their science by choosing the name according to their own individual idea of an harmonious name, forgetting that there is danger of thus interfering with the experiences that the child may get in this life. Seldom is it that any attempt is made to choose a name that contains the vibrations of the parents. Neglect of this is the cause of great estrangement in the future, since the child develops out of harmony with its parents, even though it may be under the law of harmony according to vibration.

It will be readily seen that this method of dealing with the names of children does not detract in any way from the usefulness of Numerology, but only insures the correct choice of a name by the parties who, typifying the consciousness that attracted the ego, are best qualified to indentify and extend themselves through its expression.

The name of the child should be chosen before birth since this has been proven to have the effect of causing the PATH OF LIFE vibrations to adjust themselves more in harmony with the vibrations of the name chosen, thus insuring an easier life for the child.

Lesson Eight of The Cheasley Home Study Course

CHAPTER IX

HIDDEN DESIRE OF EACH VIBRATION

In pursuing the study of Numerical vibration along the lines indicated, it may be asked why the EXPRESSION of the spelling of each Number does not agree with the Number itself, since it will be seen that one vibrates 7, two vibrates 4, etc. But it is from the spelling of the numbers that we can find the ideal of each vibration if we will add the vowels of each number. The following table will explain:

6+5=11.   Ideal of 1 = 11 = Revelation
o n e
    6=6.   Ideal of 2 = 6 = Attachment
t w o
  5+5=1.   Ideal of 3 = 1 = Individual
t h re e   (expression)
  6+3   =9.   Ideal of 4 = 9 = Universality
f o   u r
  9+5   =5.   Ideal of 5 = 5 = Self (experience)
f i v e
  9   =9.   Ideal of 6 = 9 = Universality
s i x
  5+5   =1.   Ideal of 7 = 1 = Creation
s e v e n

5+9   =5.   Ideal of 8 = 5 = Self (physically
e   i g h t   related)
  9+5   =5.   Ideal of 9 = 5 = Self (universally
n i n e   related)

CHAPTER X

HARMONIOUS ASSOCIATION.

Perhaps the most severe of life's initiations are handed to us over the line of association, since it is difficult to find any individual who cannot recall that at some stage of life they have allowed themselves to become linked in important relationships that have proved to be productive of disagreeable experiences.

In many instances a separation from these relationships has been effected and in the degree that many important lessons were learned we can label the chapter "good."

Yet again, there are still many individuals that remain in these unsatisfactory relationships, passing day by day, to the best of their understanding, the proofs of endurance that will claim their release.

Experience is a hard master if a thorough one, but the object of the enlightened truths that are slowly forcing their way through the religious education of our day, is the promise that the time is not far distant when all will learn their human lessons by the easier, if more rapid way of transmutation or the true understanding of the experiences with which the life is linked and the wisdom that will make for conscious choice for the future.

To help this time forward is one of the aims of Numerology. It teaches laws for selection in human association that are just as definite and simple as those it offers for the interpretation of the mystery of the individual Self.

We have found from the previous chapters that the numbers of the Ideality, Expression and PATH OF LIFE are the most important.

Therefore, to find the planes of complete harmony and happiness in all associations, it is necessary only to make a comparison of these vibrations in our own and another's Numberscope.

Every day we meet individuals to whom we are immediately drawn by a force which, although hard for our human minds to analyze, is nevertheless above the consideration of sex, worldly position, class or creed; in other words, they are friends before we hardly realize that fact that they are "recent acquaintances."

A comparison of our numbers would show that the Idealities (the numbers obtained from the addition of all the vowels in the baptismal or first full name) are identical.

The New Civilization fundamental of "Life in the long run"—reincarnation, applied through Numerology reveals these individuals as companions of a former existence in which the vibration that is now the mutual desire or Ideality, was being experienced as the Path of Life and expressed as the Expression.

Many harmonious friendships are formed because of the same number appearing as the Expression in two individuals. This places them in the same type, or class, of characters and insures that they will be interested to promote the development of the same general abilities.

It is not always that the same number in Expression forces two individuals into the closer relationships of love, marriage or business, because the harmony which is sensed and enjoyed is more the result of the past than a certainty of the present or a promise of future happiness, and is sufficient only to insure good fellowship and to help us recognize an harmonious friend.

For the deeper associations named, the individuals with whom we can obtain lasting harmony must have vibrations attuned to our Ideality—our inner nature. We can prove this by a comparison of our own Ideality number with that of any individual whom we know is really in sympathy with our deeper thoughts, visions and ideals and has proved their willingness to stand with us for their development, apart from how opposite to our own expression the individual may be, or how far removed from our personal life.

It is in Ideality, therefore, that the real plane of *understanding* in love, marriage and business lies; and complete happiness and confidence in either association is impossible unless harmony in this vibration obtains.

There are many associations contracted by parties whose Ideality numbers are not the same, but in these instances it is more the plane of tolerance than of complete understanding since a certain kind of compromising harmony can be maintained by each individual refraining from the display of the deeper nature with all its personal visionings, hopes and ideals. The ideals of those finding themselves in such relationships and not knowing the laws of vibration, are daily crucified and sacrificed upon the altar of misunderstanding and resistance, whereas a knowledge of such truths, and of what is more important, their discovery when the association is young, can, and does bring happiness upon the planes of harmony that caused the association to be born in the first place.

In business partnerships, the Ideality numbers play again as important a part, for the true success of the relationship here, rests with each individual who represents the organization, having the same interests at heart.

"The house divided against itself" that cannot stand is the business that has two or more partners who, however much agreement or distinct individual ability they may show in expression, misunderstand the common ideal, or are grinding the personal axe. This is invariably the case when the numbers of the individual Idealities are opposite in value.

When through a little practice with the methods suggested, we are able for ourselves to find the vibrations of a full baptismal name, and meet a person whose Expression number is our own Path of Life number, we can know that here is an individual who, however casually met, will occupy an important association in our life; because *all things,* including persons, that vibrate to our Path of Life number are expressing on their own plane the lesson we have come to learn and therefore, stand in the relation of our greatest teachers, whether they themselves realize it or not.

Associations formed as a result of this attraction, although always important are not always productive of the most complete harmony, but a comparison again of the numbers of the individual Idealities, will determine other planes of harmony outside of this attraction which future relationship can unfold.

When we meet individuals who are vibrating in Expression to our Path of Life, it is difficult for us to be content with the lighter associations; it is therefore only the knowledge of where the promise of complete and lasting harmony lies, that we can exert our power to avoid the closer ties of partnership towards which we feel the forces of experience are drawing, but which we can be sure are going to be more important than harmonious.

Inharmony is expressed where one number is even and the other odd.

Harmony is expressed where all numbers which we are comparing are identical.

Lesson Ten of The Cheasley Home Study Course. Part 2.

CHAPTER XI

COUNTRIES—CITIES—HOUSES

Countries, Cities, Houses, etc., not less than people, have characters, traits, and habits of their own.

Just as there are self-confident, vibrant individuals, there are strong, progressive, vibrant places, and as there are small, personal individuals, so there are small, personal places. Some cities and countries seem fairly to smile, and to welcome you with wide open arms, while others are glum, repellent and gloomy, like sick and disagreeable people. Again, there are dowdy cities whose appearance bespeaks carelessness, untidiness and lack of attention, while others are fashionable, up-to-date, cleanly, fully expressed and jealous of their appearance.

The vibrations of a country or city can just as easily be found as the vibrations of a person, and one has no need to enter a community, or to even hear about it, in order to know what its *Expression* is or the vibration that will be found predominating there. We are often attracted to countries, cities and houses, but when we arrive are entirely disappointed. Life among the conditions of these places is impossible to us and not at all the perfect thing we in our ignorance imagined it would be.

If we consider the Names and numbers of individuals in relation to the cities, states and countries in which they live, it will be found that in most cases the Ideality or Expression number derived by adding the numbers of all the vowels and all the vowels and consonants in its name, agrees with the Path of Life number of the Individual.

The reason for this is easily understood when we remember that the Path of Life digit is the sum total of our lesson in this life and that everything with this same vibration included or expressed can teach us our lesson.

```
  1  +  1+ 9+ 6=17=1+7=8  Ideality,
San Francisco
1 1 5  6 9 1 5 3 9 1 3 6=50=5  Expression.
```

attracts more people from all countries, who are working on a pathway of 8 and 5.

In choosing either the cities, houses, states or countries where we can be assured of the greater happiness and unfoldment, we must remember the same fundamental that we employ in choosing colors or any other expressions we desire to include from the cosmic plan, and this is, that we cannot expect to choose to *Express* through anything that is vibrating Expression to the digit of our Path of Life, because we only learn our lessons by growth and cannot jump into possession of unfoldment and be happy or successful.

Whatever is our address, number of house, name or number of street, name of city, state and country, when totaled up in vibration, will tell the effect of the whole experience we include in our unfoldment at each place in which we choose to live. The number of the house however, is the most important to consider, for the individual numbers that go to make the final digit will explain the experiences we will have, or have had in the house, just as the final digit is the real initiation under which we put our life. For instance:

253=2+5+3=1+0=1, tells us that while in this house we shall have to maintain our individuality and make unity with many new creations around our personal life which will mean surrender and adjustment, but which will pass us on to higher opportunities if we make the constructive unity with conditions=1. We also see that we shall meet all kinds and conditions of people —2, shall have changes that will be rather unexpected—5, and shall have some personal perfected expression and opportunities to develop more individual work—3.

Should we occupy rooms in such a house, that have their own numbers, we can just as easily read the smaller but closer experiences that will come around our personal work and life in those rooms.

One of the principal rules for choosing harmonious houses and rooms, is, if we are named and numbered in the even vibrations, *i. e.*, if our Ideality, Expression and Path of Life are even numbers, never to choose a house that has a number digit of an odd number, and vice versa.

Another rule is; any house or room whose number is that of our Expression we can always expect to control. In other words, we can be comfortable and able to govern the influences that will come around us while in such a home or workshop. For example a person whose Expression is 5 by the numbers 1-7-6 is harmonious in houses and rooms that vibrate 1, 7 or 5.

We must expect to be attracted to cities and countries whose Ideality or Expression number is similar to our Path of Life number as already explained, but in our choice in these directions we must see that the number of our Expression is either the same or complemental to the Expression of the city or country in which we are hoping to settle harmoniously. The only exception to this rule seems to be when choosing a town or country for a visit on entirely business purposes and in which we do not concern ourselves particularly about harmonious conditions. In this case, the Expression of the place and our own Expression may be opposite in vibration, since we contemplate such a situation only for a definite and temporary purpose.

CHAPTER XII

LIKELY OCCUPATIONS

The following are occupations that can be engaged in by, or offer the most harmonious opportunities for each vibration, according to the Number of the individual's EXPRESSION:

(1) Departmental managers, foremen, forewomen, chief clerks, military service, and any position where they have control without being the supreme authority.

(2) Builders, diplomats, politicians, corporation secretaries, corporation lawyers, salesmen, solicitors, and positions where they stand between the mass and any high authority.

(3) Ministers, designers, entertainers, secretaries, novelists, hosts and hostesses, and any position where there is not actual physical work to be done, but where they can have the opportunity to be artistic, express inspiration, and be useful in many ways by expressing themselves personally and individually.

(4) Teachers, mechanics, engineers, architects, chemists, electricians, business men, and any position where energy, intellect and physical endurance and attention to detail is required.

(5) Surgeons, Traveling salesmen, company promoters, original advertisement writers, humorists, inventors, journalists, teachers of psychology, and psychics, and any position that is not monotonous, where they have freedom and opportunity to experience travel, change, variety and originality.

(6) Heads of institutions, nurses, teachers, heads of businesses, dressmakers, housekeepers, musicians, lawyers and positions where they have the opportunity to exercise artistic ability and to be well employed.

(7) Fiction writers, clergy, organists, horticulturists, mining engineers, real estate agents, and positions where they are responsible in authority, and are brought into contact with nature and not required to do menial labor.

(8) Stock brokers, company presidents, heads of corporations, judges, printers, and positions where they have direction and control of material expression, and where their judgment of material values is accepted as final.

(9) Satirists, educationalists, writers, tragedians, specialists, healers, sculptors, players of stringed instruments, painters, reformers, criminal judges, defending counsel, founders of institutions for the care of animals, and positions where they can have freedom of thought and action, opportunity for artistic expression, sympathy, inspiration and emotion.

CHAPTER XIII

WHAT TO DO EACH DAY

If we find the vibration of each day by adding the numbers of the month, day and year, as to find the PATH OF LIFE, we can find certain things that are good to remember and apply for harmony in our life.

It will also help us to understand, by telling the force that is strongest each day, why we sometimes feel entirely unfit to accomplish the particular work we set ourselves, though we may be perfectly well physically, and the very next day perfectly able and willing to accomplish the same task.

October 15, 1915=1+6+7=14=5
October=10=1 (10th month on the calendar).
15=1+5=6
1915=1+9+1+5=16=1+6=7
1+6+7=14=1+4=5 is a 5 day when the force of 5, change, is predominating; the following table gives advice worth remembering for every day.

1—Be particular not to break any appointments, but make willing unity with everything that arises. Maintain your individuality.

2—Take every opportunity of collecting knowledge in every possible way. Be tactful and unite with all the different classes of people and conditions you may meet, whether they seem beneath you or not.

3—Don't labor on this day. Be yourself, sociable, patient and companionable. Take every opportunity of perfecting your personal expression.

4—Pay attention to detail, obey orders, and don't be afraid of hard work, intellectual or physical. Increase your knowledge of material technical expression.

5—Don't follow the beaten track of others. Be inspirational, original, ingenious, make your work interesting. Take advantage of every change that offers and turn it into a new opportunity.

6—Finish the things you undertake, and don't be afraid of responsibility or trust reposed in you. Be cheerful, keep busy, and help others.

7—Don't hustle, worry, or get excited. Take a day by yourself in the country, meditate, reflect and re-arrange your life in thought. Do things in your own way and let others do things in theirs.

8—Engage in new business. Take every opportunity that arises of increasing your physical and intellectual value. Help those under you, employ labor, and attend to your business matters.

9—Don't follow personal desire or undertake work that restricts your personal freedom. Keep your temper, express freedom in thought and action; be artistic and broad-minded.

11—Don't engage in business or spend time pursuing money. Express some revelation through usefulness. Think upon spiritual truth and endeavor to see the good in everything, disregarding influences that would bring despondency and discouragement.

22—Take every opportunity of teaching and uplifting those around you. Try to express usefulness and revelation through material, practical methods. Be ready to co-operate and to develop your ideas through demonstration and illustration.

CHAPTER XIV

NUMBERS AND PERSONALITY

As the interested reader develops into the student of Numerology, he will naturally desire to commence to apply the science as practically as he can to the conditions and people around him, in order to give him an advantage in every-day contact with life.

It is not always possible, however, to discover the vibrations of the people we meet by applying all the tests of this science that have been explained in the foregoing chapters, because it is not possible to have the opportunity of learning the full baptismal name and the birth date on first acquaintance. In order that we may still have the advantage of our knowledge, we must apply it to the only expressions a first acquaintance is likely to afford, viz., the signature and the appearance of the individual.

As regards the appearance and manner of those around us we can deduce from dress, mannerisms and peculiarities of speech, the number that is being operated as Expression or is being absorbed as Path of Life. The following table which the author has proved from his own observations to be correct, is offered as a guide to the student in making his own deductions.

IN APPEARANCE

Neat. Particular in dress, but a little severe. Dominant. Self assertive. Decided in movements.=Expression or Path of Life 1.

Plainly attired, a little careless, familiar, suave, undecided in manner, sociable, hard to take offense.=Expression or Path of Life 2.

Perfected personality, social, effervescent, accomplished, talkative; often distracting chatterers, impatient, exacting and critical; always stylishly adorned and usually good looking with small, regular features.=Expression or Path of Life 3.

Energetic, practical in dress, forceful, skeptical, materialistic, honest and direct; preference for green materials in clothes.=Expression or Path of Life 4.

Fascinating, ingenious, original, chic, amusing, obstinate, changeable, spendthrift, philanderers. Somewhat different in dress and manner. Quick response to the opposite sex.=Expression or Path of Life 5.

Substantial, conservative, cheerful, busy, quiet, unassuming, sympathy with home ties and anxious to help others. Plainly but artistically dressed, trustworthy and deliberate in manner. =Expression or Path of Life 6.

Refined, reserved, reflective, unresponsive, not very wide-a-wake in appearance and manner.

Attracted to the country, to sit quiet, to be alone. Expensive and refined in dress often preference for oriental shades and ornaments, somewhat preoccupied and pious in manner.=Expression or Path of Life 7.

Energetic, pushful, successful looking, money makers, masters of technical display. Personal in their desires, interested in spiritual and psychological subjects. Preference for green and canary colors.=Expression or Path of Life 8.

Rather ponderous, self-advertising, expressive, artistic, dramatic, ambitious, courteous, sympathetic, generous, philanthropic; anxious to create a good impression, impulsive, sarcastic, demanding self-freedom, travelers. Preference for red and orange.=Expression or Path of Life 9.

Decisive, dominant, exacting, dramatic, love of ceremony, worship and control, blunt, highly religious; particular as to their surroundings; at times foolishly generous, at others surprisingly mean. Preference for black and white.=Expression or Path of Life 11.

Diplomatic, interesting, entertaining, instructive, willing to co-operate. Variety artistes, dancers, instrumentalists. Sometimes physically limited, bad health and weak bodies.=Expression or Path of Life 22.

If the reader will memorize the above he will be able to obtain several clues to the principal vibrations of those with whom he comes in contact for the first time, and of others who are never more than his acquaintances. He will at the same time understand how to adjust himself harmoniously to those with whom his life is cast from day to day.

—THE END—

NUMBERGRAMS
by
CHEASLEY

The material sciences recognize and explain attraction and repulsion on the physical plane. Numerology recognizes and explains these laws on the psychical, mental and physical.

Numerology is new only in its modern development. Its principles were taught by the philosophers of China, Egypt, Persia, Greece and India, centuries before the Christian era.

Numerology is founded on mathematics, the basic principle of the Universe and is therefore above the danger of local color that is bound to play a part in intuitional methods of analysis.

Numerology believes that no fact can be fully understood, and consequently overcome, until we know it in its relation to the Whole.

Numerology permits of an absolutely unbiased view of the fundamental causes in every problem of life. Based on mathematics it stands as a consistent vehicle of adjustment among the inconsistencies of partial creeds, psychologies, and philosophies.

Numerology indicates the way to Health, Wealth, Love and Usefulness for each individual rather than for the human race as a whole. It believes that the true way to benefit humanity is to put the *individual* on the right track.

Numerology provides its students with a sane, practical, logical view of the realties in the problems of their own lives and the lives of others.

Numerology fills a human need because in time of trouble it offers a solution freed from the influence of personalities and traditional race thought.

Numerology is the logical study both for the beginner and the advanced student in Higher Thought. With Numerology as a background the beginner is able to measure and either reject or accept all statements made or written by subsequent teachers. The advanced student finds in it the answer to inconsistencies he has collected in his study and the revelation of Universal expression to which he has gradually been evolving.

STUDY NUMEROLOGY NOW—Cease to meet life as an accident—LIVE IT AS AN ART.

Personal Work of Clifford Cheasley

in the

Most Consistent Development

of

NUMEROLOGY

A NUMBERSCOPE tells the hidden meaning of your name and birth date,

What you want to be
What you appear to be
What you can be
What you ought to be
The lesson you came to learn
The situations to avoid
Your success attitudes.
The divine Purpose of your Life.

and many other things of vital interest to your self-development and the pursuit of happiness to which everyone is entitled.

Send for Numberscope Blank and fuller particulars

NOW

TUITION—An exhaustive Course of fourteen lessons can be taken by those desiring to become students of Numerology. Each lesson takes about one hour and the student is expected to write the important fundamentals from dictation. The working of the principle and calculation under discussion is then explained fully and demonstrated on the black board. This Course is given privately to *individuals;* not in classes except in the case of relatives wishing to take it together. It can be covered quickly or at long intervals according to the time at the disposal of each student.

At the end of this course the student receives a diploma. Those that indicate their intention of becoming teachers of the Science are given six extra lessons in teachers' practice and a final examination covering this advanced Course.

Full description of each lesson and terms on request.

CONSULTATIONS—Mr. Cheasley has adjusted successfully the personal problems of hundreds in trouble with difficulties of Health, Wealth, Love, and Work, and can be seen at all days and hours, with or without an appointment.

VERBAL ANALYSIS—This is a condensation of the Numberscope given verbally by appointment. It deals with your desires, abilities and opportunities and with pressing questions of the moment. Write for an appointment.

EXTRA SERVICE Plan—Personal attention given by attendance or by mail at reduced special fee, to those who have previously obtained a Numerscope or Verbal analysis for the purpose of direct advice and suggestion on immediate difficulties of all kinds.

FORECAST OF INFLUENCES—This is a chart containing over 2,000 words. It is helpful in developing your opportunities, explaining existing conditions and indicating changes from month to month. Written for the full calendar year, half-year, or three months.

NUMEROLOGY MONTHLY—"The Tiny Magazine with the Big Purpose" a medium by which those interested may keep in touch with the latest activities in Numerology. Carries many features of practical, worldwide and personal interest, as well as the popular lectures of Mr. Cheasley.

PUBLIC LECTURES—Given every week by Mr. Cheasley in New York, Philadelphia, and other cities. Those who send their name and address will be kept posted as to dates.

PROFESSIONAL ENGAGEMENTS—Out of town lectures, classes and analysis, to progressive centers, clubs, or study groups can be arranged on a co-operative basis.

INDUSTRIAL WORK—Mr. Cheasley has devoted much time and experiment to the selection of employees for various grades of work, and in the re-arrangement of groups of workers toward more efficient association. To the employer Numerology offers an attractive medium for better understanding of those associated with his organization, because it is the pioneer Science of CHARACTER ANALYSIS AT A DISTANCE and can be operated by direct correspondence with Mr. Cheasley, and withopt contact with the individuals analysed.

Full particulars of all of the above features will be gladly mailed and furnished

by

CLIFFORD W. CHEASLEY,
Philosopher
337 West 23rd Street, New York City, U. S. A.

www.ingramcontent.com/pod-product-compliance
Lightning Source LLC
Chambersburg PA
CBHW081257170426
43198CB00017B/2828